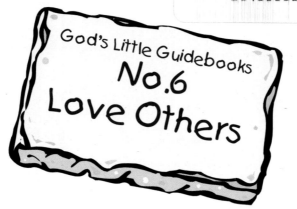

God's Little Guidebooks
No.6
Love Others

CHRISTIAN FOCUS

Sam is outside playing with his friends.
They are having fun in the garden.

Gary has brought his new football with
him.

The sun is shining brightly. Soon they are all hot and thirsty.

Sam's Dad brings them some cold
drinks and biscuits.

After a rest Sam, Scott and Rebecca
decide to play football again.

Gary decides to go home and asks for
his football back.

Scott says, 'No' and continues to play.

Gary pushes Scott - Scott hits Gary.

Soon they are calling each other names. A big fight is about to start.

Sam knows it is wrong to say horrible things and to fight.

He tries to help by giving the ball back to Gary.

Scott is in a bad mood and starts to sulk.

Their fun has been spoiled. Sam asks them both to say sorry.

The boys say sorry and soon they are all friends again.

Sam remembers God's sixth command.

Do not kill
Exodus 20:13

We can hurt people by our words and actions. God wants us to love each other.

"Let me down!"
Banana Beard
demanded. "I'll
not be a monkey
pirate prisoner!"

The ghost of Captain
Baggypants floated closer.
He drew his long sword. "Nowhere
to run, Captain Run," he said.

"It's actually Captain Banana
Beard," Fossey corrected.

"Oh, really? Well . . . good," said Baggypants. "That is a bit more fitting for a monkey pirate, for certain." He looked over his shoulder. "First Mate Topper!"

"Aye, Captain," said one of the ghost monkey pirates. He wore a ragged top hat.

"Throw them into the volcano!" ordered Baggypants. "No one comes to me island and lives to tell the tale!"

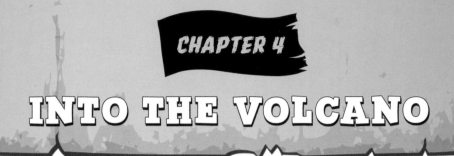

CHAPTER 4

INTO THE VOLCANO

The ghost monkey pirates drew their swords. Mr Pickles squeezed his eyes shut as they floated closer.

WHAK! WHAK! WHAK-WHAK!

The ghosts sliced through the vines holding up the monkey pirates. The prisoners fell to the jungle floor. **THUD!** They were still wrapped tightly with thinner vines.

"Ouch," said Captain Banana Beard. "That hurt a lot. So . . . I think we've learned our lesson. Haven't we, mateys?"

"Oh, yes," said Fez.

"Absolutely," agreed Fossey.

Mr Pickles nodded.

"So we'll just be on our way now," said Banana Beard.

Baggypants grinned. "I think not," he said.

The ghost pirates picked up each of the monkey pirates. They floated up over the treetops, drifting higher and higher.

The ghost pirates were nearing the top of the smoking volcano. Mr Pickles could keep quiet no longer. "Captain!" he shouted. "Permission to speak, sir?"

"You just spoke," replied the captain. "I ordered you to be quiet!"

"But I was asking permission, sir," said Mr Pickles.

"You spoke again!" said Captain Banana Beard. "This isn't like you at all, lad. Disobeying orders."

"Might as well let him speak," said Captain Baggypants. "For they be his last words."

Just then, the ghost of Captain
Baggypants grabbed Mr Pickles.
He held him over the mouth of the
volcano. Mr Pickles trembled
with fear.

CHAPTER 5

MR PICKLES AND THE MAP

"It's all my fault!" shouted Mr Pickles.

"What?" asked the ghost of Captain Baggypants.

Captain Banana Beard nodded. "It's true. There's no need to throw all of us in. He's the one who found the map!"

Baggypants squinted. "What map?" he asked.

"This one right here." The captain squirmed an arm free. He reached into his beard and pulled out . . .

"A banana?" Baggypants asked. "Who makes maps out of bananas?" He turned to Topper. "What has become of monkey pirates these days?"

"Thank you, Your Majesty," said
Banana Beard.

Baggypants held up a finger.
"But you must promise to leave
and never return."

Banana Beard nodded. "Oh, yes. But about the treasure," the captain added. "I don't suppose a group of ghosts really need gold, do you?"

"Go!" roared the ghost.

Captain Banana Beard led the way as the monkey pirates ran back to the ship.

"Just so you know, Mr Pickles," the captain said as he ran, "I'll be taking away your crayons from now on."

Mr Pickle sighed. "Aye-aye, Captain."

ABOUT THE AUTHOR

Michael Anthony Steele has been in the entertainment industry for more than twenty years. He has worked in several capacities within film and television production from props and special effects all the way up to writing and directing. For many years, Michael has written exclusively for family entertainment, including several children's television series. He has written more than one hundred books for various characters and brands, including *Batman*, *Green Lantern*, *LEGO City*, *Spider-Man*, *The Hardy Boys*, *Garfield* and *Night at the Museum*.

ABOUT THE ILLUSTRATOR

Pauline Reeves lives by the sea in south-west England, with her husband, two children and her dog, Jenson. She has loved drawing and creating since she was a child. Following her passion, Pauline graduated from Plymouth College of Art with a degree in illustration, and she specializes in children's literature. She takes inspiration from the funny and endearing things animals and people do every day. Pauline works both digitally and with traditional materials to create quirky illustrations full of humour and charm.

GLOSSARY

crumple crush something into wrinkles and folds

disobey go against the rules

dodge avoid something by moving quickly

permission allowed to do something

ragged old, torn, worn out

volunteer someone who offers to do something

SHARE WITH YOUR MATEYS

1. How would the story have been different if Captain Banana Beard had let Mr Pickles explain about the map?

2. Captain Baggypants tells Mr Pickles that he will make a "fine monkey pirate captain one day". Do you agree? Why or why not?

FOR YOUR PIRATE LOG

1. Captain Banana Beard isn't always a great leader. Make a list of qualities that you think make someone a good leader.

2. Captain Baggypants' island is haunted by magic coconuts and attacking vines. What other spooky and special things could be lurking on the island? Use your imagination and write a paragraph that describes your ideas.

3. Draw a pirate map of your school. Decide where you would bury the treasure (and what the treasure would be). Now give it to a friend and see if they can read it!

THE SHIP DOESN'T STOP HERE!

Discover more at www.raintree.co.uk